Where Truth Lies

Where Truth Lies

Poems by

Bill Christophersen

Cover design by Shay Culligan

ISBN: 978-1-950462-85-8

Kelsay Books Inc.

kelsaybooks.com

502 S 1040 E, A119
American Fork, Utah 84003

Acknowledgments

The following poems have appeared in print as indicated:

ArLiJo: "Cicadas," "January," "Mnemonic"
Blue Unicorn: "My Father's Hand"
Birmingham Poetry Review: "January," "March"
Borderlands: "Giving It Up"
Comstock Review: "Odysseus, Suspended"
Great River Review: "Still Life with Soaking Dentures"
Hanging Loose: "Mnemonic," "The Tip of the Tongue"
Hurricane Review: "October"
Kansas Quarterly: "Cropped Limes" (as "April Limes")
Light: "Lies"
Measure: "Post-Mortem"
New Orleans Review: "November"
Poetry: "February"
Potomac Review: "The Watch"
Pudding: "Pausing from Chores"
Rhino: "Pursuing the Hem of Truth into the Foothills,"
    "The Seafarer"
Right Hand Pointing: "Langur Monkeys in a Fig Tree:
    a Photograph"
South Dakota Review: "August," "Milky Way"
Tampa Review: "May," "July," "December"
Texas Review: "Ars Poetica"
Upstart: "Sleeping in Kansas"

Contents

Still Life with Soaking Dentures

The Seafarer

'Ingol... Mae *Llawlyfr ar gyfer Dolu:* cryno sy'n brin o hunandosturi ond ... ... ac yn dwymgalon. Mae'n ychwanegiad hael a phwysig at arlwy cynyddol o hunangofiannau therapiwtig sy'n ein helpu ni i ymbalfalu drwy fywyd modern'
The Sunday Times

'Mae'r llyfr yn fôr o ddeallusrwydd ond mae'n cael ei gyflwyno mewn ffordd anffurfiol, fel petai rhywun yn eistedd ar erchwyn eich gwely, yn hytrach nag yn sefyll ar lwyfan... Ceir cysur nid yn unig yn ei eiriau o gyngor, ond yn y ffordd mae'n llwyddo i gynnig sicrwydd wrth wneud hynny... Yn y pen draw, efallai na fydd modd i ni drwsio ein calonnau drylliedig ond gallwn barhau i fyw, serch hynny, a gall ein calonnau dyfu a gwerthfawrogi rhyfeddodau bywyd. Dyna sut mae'r darllenydd yn teimlo ar ôl ei ddarllen'
Matt Haig, *Observer*

'Mae'n ysgrifennu'n groyw a gydag empathi am sut i fyw gyda galar a cholled ond gan ofalu bod lle yn eich calon i obaith hefyd'
Red

'Mae Rentzenbrink wedi bod ar daith hir ac anodd tuag at ryw fath o wellhad ac yn *Llawlyfr ar gyfer Dolur Calon* mae'n rhannu'r doethineb y mae wedi brwydro mor galed amdano yn y gobaith o helpu unrhyw un sydd wedi'i lorio gan alar neu dor calon... Mae'n llyfr gwerth chweil hefyd os oes

gennych chi anwyliaid sy'n dioddef... Llyfr twymgalon, llawn ing, cydymdeimlad a gonestrwydd, sy'n cynnig cyfoeth o ddoethineb a dealltwriaeth a fydd yn gysur i eneidiau coll yn eu hangen'
Daily Express

'Ar gyfer unrhyw un a hoffai deimlo'n llai unig yn ei boen meddwl neu ei alar... map y mae'r awdur wedi ei greu yn sgil ei dolur calon ei hun i helpu eraill i sylweddoli nad ydyn nhw ar eu pennau eu hunain'
Metro

'Mae'n rhoi cyngor tawel ynghylch beth i'w ddweud wrth y rhai sydd wedi dioddef tor calon, ac yn cynnig dulliau o fynegi galar sy'n osgoi ystrydebau'
Bryony Gordon, *The Daily Telegraph*

'Geiriau doeth i helpu i'n harwain ar hyd y daith... Llyfr bendigedig, twymgalon'
Prima

'Meddyliwch am Cathy Rentzenbrink fel eich ffrind gorau newydd – cynnes, ffraeth a thu hwnt o ddoeth'
Woman & Home

'Llyfr twymgalon... canllaw cadarn i helpu unrhyw un sy'n dioddef tor calon i oroesi, neu'r sawl sy'n adnabod rhywun arall sy'n dioddef. Mae yma falm iachusol, ond hefyd doreth o ddoethineb i roi gwydnwch i rywun yn y byd go iawn'
Bookseller

'Llowciais *Llawlyfr ar gyfer Dolur Calon* mewn un darlleniad. Mae'n llawn harddwch a doethineb... dwi'n prynu copi i bawb dwi'n eu caru'
Laura Barnett, awdur *The Versions of Us*

'Mae *Llawlyfr ar gyfer Dolur Calon* yn ddoeth ac yn graff. Mae'n un o'r llyfrau mwyaf teimladwy a gonest i mi ei ddarllen erioed ac mae'n siŵr y bydd yn cynnig goleuni ym mhen draw'r twnnel i lawer o bobl. Mae'n ddewr iawn ac yn wir iawn'
Suzanne O'Sullivan, awdur *It's All In Your Head*

'Pan drodd fy mywyd wyneb i waered, dyma'r llyfr yr hoffwn fod wedi ei ddarllen. Os oes unrhyw un o'ch cydnabod wedi'i lethu gan alar, gall *Llawlyfr ar gyfer Dolur Calon* ddangos i chi sut i fod y ffrind y mae ei angen arnyn nhw'
Decca Aitkenhead, awdur *All At Sea*

'Ffrind doeth, eglur, cynnes a chynhwysol i'ch helpu drwy gyfnodau o dristwch mawr – eich tristwch chi neu dristwch un o'ch anwyliaid. Dylai'r llyfr hwn fod ar gael ar bresgripsiwn'
Sali Hughes, awdur *Pretty Honest*

'Mae *Llawlyfr ar gyfer Dolur Calon* yn llyfr a allai newid bywyd y person sy'n cydio ynddo ar yr adeg iawn. Hoffwn allu mynd yn ôl a'i roi i mi fy hun ar wahanol adegau yn fy mywyd... Mae'n cyflwyno'r neges hynod bwysig honno: dydych chi ddim ar eich pen eich hun'
Alice Adams, awdur *Invincible Summer*

'Doeth, hael, goleuni, balm, mae Cathy Rentzenbrink yn llonni'r enaid'
Megan Bradbury, awdur *Everyone Is Watching*

'Darllenais *Llawlyfr ar gyfer Dolur Calon* mewn un eisteddiad. Dechreuais feddwl y dylwn ei roi i ambell berson, y gallai helpu fy ffrind a fy chwaer, ond wedi dim ond ychydig o dudalennau, sylweddolais ei fod yn siarad â mi am yr holl adegau yn fy mywyd yr oeddwn wedi dymuno clywed gair caredig neu bwt o ddoethineb a fyddai'n fy nghynnal drwy gyfnodau anodd iawn. Dydy Cathy ddim yn therapydd nac yn feddyg ac mae'r llyfr yn well o'r herwydd. Mae'n ddynol ac yn garedig ac wedi'i wreiddio ym mywyd bob dydd, yn yr iaith rydym i gyd yn ei hadnabod ac yn yr erchyllterau sy'n gyfarwydd i bawb sydd erioed wedi teimlo allan o reolaeth neu ar goll i'r fath raddau fel nad ydyn nhw'n gallu siarad. Mae wedi fy hudo. Mae wedi fy addysgu. Mae angen copi ymhob cartref: fel tortsh a ffiws sbâr, gall eich helpu i ddod o hyd i'ch ffordd adref'
Kit de Waal, awdur *My Name Is Leon*

Llawlyfr ar gyfer Dolur Calon

Magwyd CATHY RENTZENBRINK yn Swydd Efrog a
bu'n byw am flynyddoedd lawer yn Llundain cyn
dychwelyd i Gernyw, lle cafodd ei geni.
Mae'n awdur ac yn newyddiadurwraig.
Hi yw awdur *The Last Act of Love*,
un o gofiannau mwyaf poblogaidd y
Sunday Times, a gyrhaeddodd restr fer
Gwobr Llyfrau Wellcome.

Hefyd gan Cathy Rentzenbrink

THE LAST ACT OF LOVE

City of Crystal

You'd bring a rope, a stick, a hands-free light·
ease yourself into that V-shaped rift
in the rock face overshadowing the creek.
Inside, a clammy, claustrophobic flue
descends gradually, describes a lazy arc,
then opens out, as limestone often will.
There, emerging from a yellow-gray
mineral incrustation, glazed and wet,
quartz prisms rise, chock-a-block—
some parallel, some askew; protrude
into a natural vault. You're ogling
a cityscape of amaranthine-blue
blown glass—and wondering what else
the been-here-done-that world has up its sleeve.

Where Truth Lies

Lies

When I was young, it tickled me to lie.
"Does your Mom know you're skipping school today?"
"Of course she does. She said, 'Be sure to stay
in this adult movie house till I come by
and pick you up.'" I'd give the truth a try
from time to time, but much preferred to play
the juggler, juggling facts in artful ways
to make some cockamamie story fly.
But that was yesterday. Enough's enough.
Though poetry offers license to deceive,
to fib and fudge, invent and feign and bluff,
I'd rather not. I no longer believe
half of what I read, much less the stuff
I hear. Lying's abused. Truth needs a reprieve.

Shoebox Spectroscope

My ninth-grade science
project was a shoebox
rigged at one end with
razor blades taped side
by side over a hole cut
in the cardboard to form
a narrow aperture for light.
At the other end and
similarly installed, a
grating—a prismatic
window—resolved the
incoming beam. You'd
close one eye, put the
other to the grating, and
there inside the box—a
band of unbraided colors.
Daylight's rainbow was
only the beginning. At
night I trained the device
on the neon tube light of
McGillicuddy's: a bar
code of red and orange
lines. Argon, mercury
vapor, tungsten filament
and fluorescent light—
each displayed its
signature hues. I had
penetrated the appearance
of things, eyeballed their
essences. I envisioned
demonstrating my device
to this girl or that, "Here,
close one eye and put the
other to the grating;

now look at that
streetlight. . . ."
                    I still
have the contrivance,
its black contact paper
curling at the edges.
The spectroscope has
reverted to shoebox. I
take it down from the
closet shelf, blow off
the dust. Inside:
rent receipts from '75,
a torn letter, a
red rabbit's foot.

Post-Mortem

She wasn't like my Norwegian grandma: fun-
loving, indulgent, proffering snacks and sips
of lemonade. This one pursed her lips;
scowled; cinched her hair in an airtight bun
and, Scottish burr sizzling on her tongue,
scolded her daughter for catering to my whims
at suppertime. "He's no' the royal scion,"
she'd snort, then filch my last potato chip.
I didn't care for her staying at our place.
Didn't care for her veined, rice-paper skin,
the lump on the side of her neck, her turtle chin,
the not-quite-with-it looks that crossed her face,
the old-apartment odor of her breath.
Spoiled child, I refused to partake of my Grandma's death.

The Wheel

Not far from Thomsonville, New York,
a rider-less Ferris wheel revolves
at the top of a hill—advertisement
for an amusement park that otherwise
can't be seen from the interstate.
Summer nights, motorists try to
keep one eye on the road as the other
strays, mesmerized by the green-
and-yellow wheel's floodlit revolutions.

*

For weeks we'd seen that ectoplasmic
halo hovering beyond the town.
After graduating, six of us
launched a fact-finding expedition.
Spent the day there; blew our wad
on rides, hover ball, arcades,
beer and pizza burgers. Buzzed,
we watched night fall, a Strawberry Moon
climb the roller coaster's silhouette.

Eventually, I and a blonde whose name
I forget climbed the weedy hill
to see the Ferris wheel up close—its
electron cloud of moths, its perfect
silence, the amusement park
a video game playing itself below. . . .
At the arc's low point, the cars
wafted past no more than eight
feet above the packed-gravel base.

19

I didn't know from girls—didn't know
from much, really. What's 18?
Feature-length daydreams, fantasies
of dying heroically, riptide
of desires, the urge to solo on
some musical instrument yet to be
taken up. . . . On an impulse,
I winked, turned, leapt and caught
the undercarriage of an approaching car.

During most of that endless-seeming
revolution, I prayed like any
teenage nut-job who's put his life
in hock for a lark, a dare, the need
to wow someone he's scared to even
speak to; pleaded with the God
whose amusement our shenanigans
provide to just this once indulge
my dip-stick prank; to spare my dip-stick life.

Gravity almost undid me, prying
hand and finger muscles. Fear
was a tangy nausea; inward
scream segueing to limbic drone.
Come full-circle, I couldn't undo
my convulsive grip on the bar; overshot;
wrenched myself free; landed hard
on my back—a stunned bug, spasming,
some part of me still wedded to the wheel.

*

The girl was amazing: very together.
Don't move. Lie down flat. What's
my name? Made me promise not
to budge while she ran for help. I
was out of it. In pain, of course,
but more than that: I was still aloft,
moths grazing my face, footlights
giving me the third degree:
Who are you, kid? Where was your brain tonight?

Nothing was broken. My sprained back hurt
like hell for weeks, but after it healed,
I walked on air for a month—then fell
into a bear-trap funk. Other guys
enlisted, took factory jobs,
strapped themselves into something tight:
marriage, mortgage, long commutes.
I was having none of that.
Killed time at the park. Got good at hover ball.

I sometimes wished I was back in school
where I knew the drill. What happened next:
To make a little cash, I took
a job installing drywall. Right—
with my back! Was I crazy? Build
some muscles, is what I was thinking. Then
one day I'm hanging a wall and the girl
from the park walks in! She's subleasing,
doing freshman orientation at State college.

She'd come to think of me as another
James Dean. Which was fine with me.
I'd been fooling with the theory that
you are who people think you are.
Our fling was short: I'm James Dean Lite
at best, with a couple quarts of Sal
Mineo thrown in. On top of that,
the girl's main squeeze came back to town
from his internship at a Manhattan law firm.

Sorry. I made that last line up.
In fact, he'd spent the past two months
registering voters in Mississippi.
(This was 1964,
the year Chaney, Schwerner and Goodman
were killed.) I thought hard about that
as my romance cratered. I was no
politico, but I had to admit,
there was no contest. The better man had won.

*

Feeling like some low-grade ore—
a base metal in need of smelting—
I packed my bag; hit the road.
Kept a journal to give my thoughts
a place to mature, to muster up.
Got work driving an ice cream truck
in a suburb of Denver. Spent a month
teaching Arapahoe kids to spell.
That's when Uncle Sam caught up with me.

Served for the next couple of years
as a supplies sergeant in Guam.
It wasn't bad. I had plenty
of down time, so I read a lot:
history, fiction, biography, pop
science. I was going to college,
you might say, on my own version
of the G.I. Bill. My visiting
lecturers were guys back from the front.

A lot of these guys went to Nam
the way I hopped the Ferris wheel:
What the hell? Recruiter says
the country needs us; Asia's awash
in communism, socialism,
atheism, spoonerism;
strike a blushing crow for freedom;
do Saigon—and the Asian chicks;
make history—and the Asian chicks.

The guys I saw came back talking
crotch rot, swamp adders, night patrol,
tiger cages. They talked about
tunnel complexes blown, scouted;
the sweet and sour taste of fear;
what napalm versus white
phosphorus does to human skin;
what a torched village smells like;
One talked about what he'd done to a VC prisoner.

I'd been spared the infantryman's
black sabbath. All the same,
I came home changed. But changed is
as changed does, and I didn't do
shit. McCarthy opposed the war.
I could have volunteered, gone door
to door. We've been lied to and had,
I could have said . . . to red-faced World
War Two vets, who would've cleaned my clock.

*

Back home, I looked up friends. The girl
had moved. One friend had lost a leg.
Another'd been killed in a firefight
near Pleiku. Others' hands were tied,
working, raising families. I
vegetated for a while, then met
a guy who was writing songs, performing
at a coffeehouse. His songs
rang true; he wasn't pulling any punches.

His act, though, was kind of thin:
acoustic guitar and a reedy voice.
What I could use, he thought out loud,
is a bassist. I wasn't doing much,
so I bought a bass and started taking
lessons, practicing scales, the circle
of fifths, developing calluses,
learning to read. It kept me sane
while I tried to figure out my crazy life.

Eventually, it became my crazy
life. Back then, coffeehouses
were multiplying. Rents were low.
Gigging twice a week, I took
part-time work as a stock clerk in
a bookstore—easy, mindless stuff.
Between the two, I just about made
my bare-bones nut. I had to laugh.
My marginal tack was keeping me afloat.

The bookstore gig gave out. A bigger
bookstore came to town and grabbed
the textbook trade. I started backing
folksingers 50 miles away—
Have Bass, Will Travel;
thirty, thirty-five bucks a pop.
Got steady work with a holdout cover
band: "Young Girl," "Good Lovin',"
"Groovin'," "Satisfaction," "Turn Turn Turn."

Bassists do all right when it comes to
getting work. You don't have to be
a genius. Competent will do,
especially if you can get along
with bigger egos. The rock band gigs
took a toll on the hearing but
paid the rent. Then too, the social
scene, especially in the college towns,
was cool—sometimes a magic carpet ride.

*

Things fall apart. The Summer of Love
went to hell; rock and folk got old.
Country, on the other hand ("three
chords and the truth"), had staying power.
I've retailed Hank and Merle and Buck
and George for years—a rounder's meal
ticket, courtesy of laborers
who like their Jack, their Maker's Mark
chased with a splash of pedal steel and fiddle.

In short, I've managed to keep my seat
on this honky-tonk merry-go-round.
I won't complain, although the years
have left me little to put aside
(even assuming this old boy
had the discipline to bank a buck).
You know, the freakin' teeth will jack
you up! I damn near had to sell
the car to get a molar root-canaled.

Never married. Ask me why,
I couldn't tell you. Worked at night,
chased the outlaw thing (you don't
see Waylon Jennings settling down!).
Could be I'm constitutionally
afraid of it—that's probably closer
to the truth. But then, who's to say?
Given the right woman, the right
situation, the right economy, I might

. . . oh, invent a whole different bunch
of excuses. Hey, just keeping *myself*
in pasta, beer and granola bars
is challenge enough! The brass ring?
Let somebody else give it a lunge. . . .
My back—not that you've asked, and I
appreciate your tact—never did
heal completely; every five or six
years (these days, it's more like every

five or six months), it seizes up
and lays me out. Percocet's
addictive, but a flaring disk
will break you—medieval pain—
and I'm no everlovin' Braveheart. . . .
A week ago, I motored past
the amusement park. The wheel still turns
on top of the hill. By day, it's nothing
special. Coming home, I took a detour.

Consequences

You didn't pay attention when you left your apartment, and now the door's unlocked and you don't know whether you forgot to lock it or someone, probably armed, is inside cleaning you out.

The violin lacked a finish, but you bought it anyway because the unvarnished wood resonated in a way that made tunes leap, raw-boned, from its strings. So you threw your money away, because the box cracks anew with every shift in the weather and the luthier won't even repair it anymore.

You speed-read the opening chapters, and now you don't know who any of the characters are, much less what's going on.

You accepted the position; now the company owns you.

You turned it down, and now your Protestant conscience is calling you irresponsible and your co-op is tacking a late fee onto this month's maintenance debit.

You didn't have the scratch, so you missed the chance to see Joe Venuti at the Blue Note. Though it's also true that, had you seen the show, you would have missed the basketball game on the corner of Sixth and West 3rd, in which the skins pulled off back-to-back alley-oops.

You kissed her once, and now she expects you to kiss her again, your ambivalence notwithstanding. That ambivalence, of course, is the result of a string of sour romances, themselves the result of the usual emotional give-and-take compounded by your own sad neuroses. And now, fury at the psychological baggage you carry around is making you kiss her again—and resent her for complying (although you would resent as well her not complying).

The poem was bad, so you tore it up, even though it was your first serious effort, and now all you can remember about it is that it concerned watching the sun set over the Cross Bronx Expressway one evening in the summer of your seventeenth year, when your thoughts were full of love and death, and the setting sun became a correlative for both. That, and using the word "suffusing" to describe what the "saffrons" in the west were doing. So maybe tearing it up wasn't such a bad idea. You don't need to have your nose rubbed in that, especially now when such memories inspire so many of your current, less obviously bad poems.

You didn't want to lie when she said, "Tell me the truth," so you told her the truth. Then the only one you had to lie to was yourself.

The Right Thing

We try to say the right thing, but we fail
as often as not, the lofty sentiment
cloying, the plain truth turning tail
in the crunch. . . . The letter left unsent—
concessive handshake never quite extended;
the words of love that curdled in the throat
when constitutional reticence blended
with inveterate mistrust; the off-key note
of schadenfreude that marred the frank reply;
the overzealous thanks that sounded feigned;
the stupid joke that wounded on the fly;
the confession that embarrassed as it pained:
We try to say it right but get it wrong,
flummoxed singers butchering the song.

The Rise of the Novel

It was an age of literacy and burghers:
the one a Promethean heist, the other
an urban phenomenon that wanted its picture taken. Hence
the novel, with its novel orientation:

parlors. (The picaro? Faugh!—a kind of naughty brother.)
Soon crying was the rage all over Europe
and everyone was obsessed with the figments of somebody else's
imagination. Chandlers came into their own.

Lens grinders saw business multiply. And for what?
A vital shift in pronouns and prerogatives
couched in illicit missives, images of flying helmets.
This eighteenth-century equivalent of headphones

snared young and old, father and daughter alike
in the prehensile spasms of the nouveau riche, dark
vapors, the throes of oedipal jousting. Social commentary
came later—an excuse for all the lying.

Krapp's Anniversary Tape

She: Yesterday I was a milkshake in an earthquake.
      Today I'm a plum in hot buttered rum.
He: Yesterday I was a flake, a clotheshorse and a rake.
      Today (thanks to you) I've ditched that bum.

She: Yesterday I was a butterfly in a field of rye.
      Today I'm a moth in a dense bolt of cloth.
He: Yesterday I was a spry, sexy guy.
      Today I'm a sloth. A balding sloth.

She: Yesterday I loved you like a sweater.
He: Today we know better.

Being Here Now

How to quit the past, where I tend to dawdle
like a box turtle traversing a backyard,
and rivet myself to the here-and-now, in which
backyards are sinkholes waiting to implode?
I try not to go AWOL; try to get
my mind around today, which I know is just
a continuation of yesterday, a picture-perfect
May morning on which joggers in headphones
jog the paths in Riverside, the weather blimp
maneuvers above the Hudson, and a *Times*
Metro article reports how a Brooklyn man
and woman miffed over a stolen bag of weed
tied a boy, 14, to a chair in the basement of an
abandoned apartment building in East New York
and beat him to death with an aluminum baseball bat.

Where Truth Lies

You come across it sometimes cleaning house:
the dust ball with the miniature claw protruding
from the gluey, unconscionable rat-trap wedged behind
the stove. Or—pop goes the weasel!—there it is
disporting itself as you enter your shared apartment,
the prim roommate and her orange-haired partner
splayed like Komodo dragons across the futon,
all writhing limbs, flushed faces, bare arms groping
ludicrously for the balled-up sheet. The truth
is nesting in the eaves of the dog house gone to wrack
that you figure to demolish, such an eyesore:
the cauterizing needle in the forearm,
mud daubers strafing your unsuspecting jaw.
It takes so many forms, one hesitates
to identify it; hesitates, certainly,
to put in a good word for its protean character.
But, truth is, now and again its idle foot
will tickle yours in the library reading room
(where all those feet left alone on the carpeted floor
underneath the table strewn with books
take on lives of their own as the hours pass).
Truth bides its time in the hollow of a thigh
(that pressure point Old Testament angels fret
when street fights go against them); lets out its breath
in the cicada-riven aftermath of taps
at a veteran's funeral; proclaims itself
in the natural science article documenting
the olfactory imprinting of salmon trout;
springs, epiphanic, from the White Sale catalog
whose cornball blurb, misread, transmogrifies
into an indictment of your most irresponsible indiscretion.

Truth operates along the border of sleep; conceals itself
in dream—the recurring one, for instance, in which
you're driving up the on-ramp of a bridge
when the horizon oscillates, and suddenly you're careering
toward a wall of oncoming traffic. (Prophecy? Parable?
Not necessarily. Dreams are elusive. Like brides,
they come with layers of elaborate packaging. You'll
want to note their mise en scène and the most preposterous
association that flits across your mind the following
morning at the breakfast table as you mull
their incoherent scenarios, become obsessed
with the many anxieties that, in sickness as in health,
go to bed with you, make you, unmake you.) Truth lies
in the guest room; the back bedroom. Truth lies
underneath the bed. The bed you lie in.

Spring Cleaning

Beneath the shag rug—
the vanished salamander's
sooty skeleton.

A Defense of Poetry

A dicey task, you say. "The simple truth:
We make our way quite swimmingly without it.
What's to be gained by blathering about grief,
loss, bliss, the birds, the abyss, a rose?
We triumph, fail, hate, transcend, fear . . .
So what do we want? Gold stars? A Purple Heart?
What's the point? To get it all by rote?"
And yet, there should be *someone* taking note.

A good amanuensis would record
the flabby jogger huffing through the grove,
the second-grader prematurely bored,
the divorced husband struggling with a stove;
the ER intern walking home at night
down streets where push is wont to come to shove;
a wounded helicopter pilot's fright;
the perverse biochemistry of love.

This scribe should be a sort of chloroplast
absorbing and refining life's exhaust,
recycling its light. He should work fast,
transmogrifying some of what's been lost
into something easier to breathe—
something fresh yet inconspicuous—
so that we neither forget ("Go not to Lethe . . .")
nor wax cynical, suicidal, acrimonious.

His subject should be every little thing
that rankles, every news report with legs,
every succulent rumor on the wing
or self-debunking anecdote that begs

retelling, every Appalachian song
sung a cappella by a stone-faced maid
who neither sways nor simpers, lest she wrong
the tale by making it a serenade.

His beat should range from parking lot to playground,
cafeteria to industrial park.
His poetry should be a lost-and-found
replete with unmatched gloves, used slide rules, shark-
tooth amulets, milk cartons, rhythm sticks;
a grab-bag of taxidermy tools, string ties,
metallurgy monographs, toothpicks,
junked alternators, oriental dyes—

the thing itself. But not *only* the thing itself:
the thought that plays in the shadow of the thing
or notices its odd consortium on the shelf.
Associations, recollections, ping-
ponging wordplays, visual puns—the stuff
and nonsense of a mind on autoplay
or idly registering the dicker and chuff
of an invisible world occasionally made

in its guise beyond the window blind's dark slats
or scented as the tea ball's scalded leaves
foliate in tinctures, brick-red mattes,
plumes silking from the aluminum sleeve's
perforations—fluidities buoyed up
a second, maybe two, till they disperse:
A poem that steeps an aromatic cup
or whiffs the realm beyond is welcome verse.

Reporter, transformer, conjuror, medium . . . "Scribe,"
then, hardly tells the half of what we need
a poet for. We need a satirist to gibe
and shame power brokers into heed-
ing a less ruthless muse; a doorman to slide
back doors that frighten; an oracle to speak
riddles to the overeducated; tid-
ings of hope to hearts tied to the stake;

self-help to visionaries nickel-and-dimed
by bureaucrats; horse sense to those too prone
to dream; epiphanies to those whose rhyme-
less days are a blur of answering the phone,
attending meetings, speed-reading the news;
resilience to the teen browbeaten beyond tears;
solace to the nonagenarian who rues
the loss of loved ones steamrolled by the years.

It has its work cut out, then, poetry.
It's not at all the quaint, vestigial lobe
we sometimes take it for, that cannot be
of service anymore. (The ghost of Job
haunts the burial site of J.S. Mill.)
Leave aside the index of usefulness,
however, gold calf that it is: There's still
the urge to sing/ chant/ curse/ demand redress/

gainsay/ grouse/ invoke/ elucidate. . . .
But why go on? Why beat a living horse?
We wrangle words to speak our piece to fate;
set records straight; help us stay the course.

We do without those words the way a child
does without milk: Our health is hurt, our growth
stunted, our potential unfulfilled.
We want our lives to matter. We are loath

to see them thrown under the bus, untold.

Pursuing the Hem of Truth into the Foothills

Cokes, on the gimpy ranch? Or
cleave the bluff decorum?
Dusk brazed the backyard fence, where remnants of
Winter looms.
"Look alive!" rasped a jackleg preacher hawking
Pentecostal ultimatums.

Row, O row your favorite skull.
Shun mind and the limits of comfortable sleep
and warriorship. Good boots go far,
and buttered rum, so plug away
or, better still, Write from that not-so-crass land;
hope grows from the plucked-out orb.
The lure: a cheeky saboteur in white,
hanging from a trestle by a nostril.

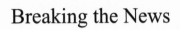
Breaking the News

Breaking the News

"In a pig's eye," she cries, and dies. . . .
Is all this mortal foofaraw a joke?
Snatching the nearest thing to bolster composure,
you sputter maledictions at the moon;
down phenobarbital, warm milk, a bromide.
How to break such inauspicious news?

The enterprising journalist makes the news.
(Everybody lies; what of it?) We all die
bug-eyed in the end, so stick to the bromide
of your choice, a racy paperback, wry joke,
banana daiquiri tinged with crescent moon-
light. . . . The main thing is to preserve composure.

That, or seek the truth and forget composure:
Scrutinize newsfeeds. Parse the evening news.
Decide for yourself whether there's life on the moon.
Fact-check the obituaries: Who really died?
Cull the running from the standing jokes
whose feet are shot. Console yourself with a bromide.

When you wake, embrace this undervalued bromide:
Truth is the stranger fiction. . . . Composure
must yield to nimbler attitudes, blacker jokes,
so deep-six it! Twig to something new.
Take up the flugelhorn before you die.
Take a sextant to the gibbous moon.

Resurrect your grad-school thesis: "The Moon
as Romantic Fallacy, Lyrical Bromide,
Nothing More Than Toasted Rock." Die
once, and the truth comes clear: Composure,
like retirement, is overrated. (Who knew?)
Shun absolute zero. Sling a joke!

Or can't *Il Penseroso* take a joke?
Perhaps he'd rather watch TV and moon. . . .
Turn off the tube. Get dressed! Forget the news—
coiffed anchorpersons, shopworn quips and bromides.
Grab the reins; kick out the footlights of composure.
Take a chance, Mr. Binge-Thinker! Shoot the die.

He who dies gets the joke.
Composure suffers; but life on the moon
is better than a bromide. No news is good news, anyhow.

Easter Bonnet

Gossamer sombrero?
Cirrocumulus halo?
The planet Saturn
encircles your brow. . . .

No matter: Your dark
hair hanging straight
under all that hat
astonishes, enthralls,

evoking as it does
the black-and-white
photograph of a
hybrid humanoid

jellyfish bobbing, list-
less, in a windless bay.
But now the daft
season's dishing up

a pastel windfall that
all but snow-globes you
in your rice-paper cum
cloud-cover coiffure, and

it's chalk up another
equinoctial haymaker,
this one replete with
debutante flying saucer.

If Your Dog Eats Grass, Do This

Immerse dog in warm tub of chlorinated mineral water. Raise and gently palpate forepaws while intoning *The grass is the flag of my disposition* in a Whitmanesque stentorian. Allow week for charm to work. If disorder persists, follow these American Veterinary Medical Association–approved behavioral reinforcement ploys:

At the stroke of midnight, suspend dog in breeder's harness from a lightning-riven sycamore. Release 500 bioluminescent moths in the immediate vicinity, while streaming Orson Welles's narration of "The War of the Worlds." (If dog appears dangerously entranced or becomes catatonic, use dropper to administer half ounce of Red Bull or comparable energy drink to counter sensory overload.)

Don faux executioner's hood. As moon rises, shampoo dog with ginger beer laced with bitter oleander. As dog shakes dry, sprinkle confectioner's sugar over its rump with one hand while shaking a pebble-filled coffee can to a Bo Diddley beat with the other.

Invite the grandkids to dress dog up in petticoats and Mardi Gras beads, then tease it with feather dusters, finger puppets and remote-controlled drones. (NB: This procedure warrants supervision.)

If disorder persists, hold croquet tournament on front lawn while "seeding" back with a dozen pelican lawn ornaments. The resulting territorial infringement combined with canine tinnitus caused by the repeated *thunk* of wooden mallets striking croquet balls should induce dog to prefer the great indoors for the foreseeable future.

Should all else fail, don scuba gear and pace back and forth in front of dog house, cutting the occasional caper, while an aide generates sporadic gastrointestinal rumblings on an amplified didgeridoo. At this point, even the most compulsive grass-eater (as well as the nosiest neighbor) will get religion and cry holy.

Getting a Read

"Read my lips," she'd seemed to say,
sauntering by.
I wasn't sure. I'd heard her out of the
corner of my eye.
"Come again?" queried my raised
brow, my glance.
"You heard me right," she winked, as I
looked askance.
She smiled then—"Another time, perhaps"—
and walked away.

My illiteracy at reading lips
had lost the day.

Use words, we tell our little ones,
so they'll be smart
and succeed in a Cartesian world.
But the heart
channels the hoary limbic node,
not Descartes.
It doesn't talk; it tweets. Its songs
are worlds apart
from the cerebrum's syntaxes.
Our excess gray

matter blunts its inflections, arpeggios,
rondelets.

Beauty

I discovered it one August afternoon
in a quarry of gray rocks. Some of them,
I'd been told, were geodes—jewels in the wild.
Crack the right one with a hammer: inside
were cities of amethysts. I spent three hours
filling a burlap sack with shattered rocks,
their petrified fruit pitted with purple crystals;
imagined setting up a glass display case—
fluorescent lights, labeled specimens. . . .
The sun got to me. A pair of yellowjackets
started strafing me. Time to go. I grabbed
the sack. It wouldn't budge. The yellowjackets
had my number. I snagged my father's hammer
and one geode, and got the hell out of there.

Sixteen

Girlfriend flirting with
best buddy . . . The Sturgeon Moon
washes up, gray-white.

The Tip of the Tongue

Just there, ensconced
among taste buds: a
mite-size twilight zone,
inside which the familiar
dons a mustache and
disappears, winking.

Tease; flirt; juvenile
delinquent—ambushing,
roughing up, holding
hostage the name of my
modern fiction prof, my
freshman roommate, that
wiry, hits-to-all-fields
Yankee second-baseman
back in the late '80s,
the page-turner I finished
reading just last week. . . .

I touch it with an index
(would it had one!), as if
to tap the button that
releases memory, sends
the recalcitrant name
down the shoot like a
charm or gumball, but
the machine's gummed
up; the charm's broken.

Perverse jump stick
into which yesterday's
files, yesteryear's file
folders, vanish but *not*
without a trace (hard

drive compromised,
not crashed)—sure to
pop up later when the
operating-system-
software-interface
sorts itself out.

The tip of the tongue: no
anatomical appurtenance,
of course—just a figure
of speech subverting
speech, necessitating
figure. . . .

Old man's nematode
—I mean nemesis . . .
Memory's prostate . . .
Sand trap threatening
to engulf the course . . .
Speech impediment
that renders us dumb . . .
The null set we conned
in AP algebra: that
Boolean absurdity we
riffed on ("If I'm null,
you're void"), into which
we've begun to vanish.

Pop's Ramble

I was sixteen—a no-count harrier—the day
I passed that clutch of fagged-out quarter-milers
and chased the leader down the straightaway.
See me gut it out and break the tape?
Tendinitis, plantar fasciitis
spoiled my running game. . . . Flaccid biceps
and triceps shame me now, never mind I held
my gym class record for push-ups, pull-ups, chin-ups.
See this? Can't hardly manage—I'll be switched!—
to raise this balky sash. . . . Pass the ashtray.
Some molar's always crumbling. . . . Guess this coot's
grown tedious, eh? Stick around, see the old man
knuckle under to a midday nap and dreams
of ponytails, penny loafers, sock hops.

For John Keats

26 Piazza di Spagna. Saturday, 9 December, 1820. *In a dismal
spirit of despair, Keats contemplates suicide. Severn now takes
"every destroying means from his reach," including the laudanum
that should and could have helped him to an easeful death like Tom's.
For nine days Keats coughs up blood, . . . repeatedly enduring the
horrors of drowning and suffocation as the disease makes cavities
in his lungs and corrodes his arteries.*

—Nicholas Roe, *John Keats*

You didn't buy the teleology
that said this life's a lice-infested bed
in which we toss; a vale of tears that we—
shoeless, hapless pilgrims—can but tread,
steadied by the vision of the cross
on which a gentle soul was nailed; and by
the hope of a blissful afterlife, the loss
of which, should we despair, doubt, deny,
would relegate us to eternal pain. . . .
You posited instead a "working brain"
wrangling meaning from insignificance;
a soul distilled from rank experience. . . .
Your friends saw to it that you ended well.
To save the soul you'd painstakingly made
they took away the laudanum and bade
you die in God's good grace—that is, in hell.

Still Life with Soaking Dentures

Ars Poetica

A poem should not mean
But be.
—Archibald MacLeish, "Ars Poetica"

Forget globed fruit, palpable and mute.
A poem should hoot,

Be loud
As a pit-bullfight crowd,

Plangent as a paving stone
Smashing the casement where the Missus lodges.

A poem should mince words
Like scrapping birds.

*   *   *

A poem should fly in the face of time.
If the moon climbs,

Tail it, by God, until it wheezes.
Twig by twig, night mangles the trees,

Leaves the loon grieving, scatters the leaves
Of Memory as it pleases. . . . A poem

Should slice through space and time
And stop on a dime.

*   *   *

A poem should not be but do. A
Toadstool can be, or a blob of goo

Congealing on an engine manifold. A poem should do
Work in the old

Newtonian sense—force displacing mass.
A poem should haul ass,

Not let its pinions rust;
Should vanish in a cloud of dust.

*   *   *

Nor is its business to eschew
The *outré* and the *incongru:*

The well-groomed thug; the well-bred thief;
The afterlife of a shucked belief;

A left hand sweltering in an asbestos glove,
Inept at love.

The poem is neither beautiful nor true
Whose whiskers aren't askew.

*   *   *

Its paradigm should be a kangaroo
Cavorting, leaping walls:

A pair of outsized haunches, it should sprawl
And gangle, veer and moo.

Nor ought it be obliged to cull
False from True

Or In-Between: a poem
Is not a polygraph machine.

*   *   *

A poem should neither be
Nor mean,

Dovetail nor
Congrue,

Adjudicate nor
Construe:

A rat without a tail, a poem
Should do.

January

Here's to the god that looks both ways: behind
to evening shadows on the noonday street;
ahead to daylight-saving time, upbeat
forecasts, the fantasy that all will find
restored to them what's died, dried up, gone gray.
God of terminus *and* god of hope—
for that's the trick, isn't it? To cope
with one at night and glimpse the other by day,
so that this winding sheet of ice and snow
doubles as cocoon; so that this white
light that pains the eye and numbs the soul
disperses to reveal an Armory Show
of colors cavalcading out of sight;
so that the old year takes but its rightful toll.

Wind-Chill Factor

Wind turns twelve degrees
to two. Young suburbanite
walks her dog by car.

Peekskill traffic lights vogue in the wind,
a jangled charm bracelet.

At the Croton train station, commuters
crowd beneath yellow heat lamps—so many
French fries at the fast-food franchise.

Step off the train: air like an oxygen tent
takes your breath away. A gust from Hell Gate
(Dante's ninth circle is a polar vortex)
sucker-punches you, then laughs.

A buddy from Indiana tells me the mid-Atlantic states
don't know from cold. "Cold," he says, "is when you
jump in your car and the plastic seat covers shatter."

(The coldest I've ever been was a Christmas Eve
in Niagara Falls. We took a walk at midnight.
Three feet of snow. Half the Falls were ice.
Foggy clouds rolled up from the chasm, glazing
each twig, every bush. I was hatless—each
hair on my head a light-gauge icicle.)

The plate-glass bus shelter on 125th lies in smithereens, so
there's no respite. Nearby doorway's full of huddlers.
The wind finds an ear canal and drills. *Factor that!*

In the 1950s, there wasn't any "wind-chill factor." Minimalist forecasts ("low teens and windy") got the job done or didn't.

How do they do the math? Or is it just dueling thermometers?

Walking up Broadway
I side-step a skateboarder
in a polo shirt.

Breakfast Haiku

The morning paper
beckons, then repels. Like love.
Like Belgian waffles.

Kitchen banshee? The
old kettle screams. What does it
know that we don't know?

We toast two scones. They
hiss like feuding cats before
springing at my face.

Pour the tea: black leaves
swirl and fall—an infrared
video of sleep.

A lemon seed slides
down the side of the porcelain
cup. A bitter tear?

February

The cold grows colder, even as the days
grow longer, February's mercury vapor light
buffing but not defrosting the bone-white
ground, crusty and treacherous underfoot.
This is the time of year that's apt to put
a damper on a healthy appetite,
old anxieties back into the night,
insomnia and nightmares into play;
when things in need of doing go undone
and things that can't be undone come to call,
muttering recriminations at the door,
and buried ambitions rise up through the floor
and pin your wriggling shoulders to the wall;
and hope's a reptile waiting for the sun.

Timing

It was an old apartment. The forked lightning
of cracked plaster was everywhere, each wall
a jigsaw puzzle of hairline fractures. But the super
said it was structurally sound, even if the paint
was cracking, and I wanted to believe him.
One day I went to work and came home to find
a chunk of plaster, maybe twenty pounds,
atop my pillow, and a hole, three feet by four,
gaping overhead. In the comedy of life,
timing is everything. The mid-February warm front
that swept the Tennessee Valley states last week
spawned tornadoes in the county where my sister
lives. One tore up the women's college, demolishing
the recently completed building housing labs
for the physiology and kinesiology department—the building
in which my sister, who's majoring in kinesiology,
has a Monday evening class. The storm hit
Sunday evening. No students hurt, although
half a mile away, mobile homes were rolled
like dice; houses blown apart; people killed.
What can you say? We close our eyes, play
the percentages, stroke a rabbit's foot, pretend
we're special, saved, blessed. In a recurring dream
I'm standing on an apron of lawn that's a regular
minefield of vespiaries. C'mon in, my friends
call blithely, waving from the screened-in porch.

The Ubiquity of Marble

Midtown office restroom: marble tiles.
(Each one suggests a photographic slide
of cell tissue, where nuclear structures glide
and stream in a murky plasm.) Square miles
of such surfaces extend, citywide:
We walk upon them in museums, halls
of justice; encounter them on lobby walls
in prewar apartment buildings, on the side
panels of vestibules, concourses; see
them without seeing them, their neutral tones
surrounding us, unobtrusive, unremarked—
quaint decor; fusty panoply;
chaste masonry—until a stone
slab cracks, the splay irreparable, stark.

March

Wherein the lion and the lamb don't quite
lie down together, as the Bible prophesies,
but, in a manner of speaking, fraternize:
spar, feint and posture on the tight
canvas of late winter until the one
calls it quits and the other, stunned and wet,
wobbles through residues of snow beset
by a smell—crabgrass warming in the sun.
The plot, then: Nature pivots on a dime.
But as the ides impend, subplots abound.
No emir, sultan, president or prime
minister but keeps an ear to the ground.
Coup? Cabal? Arab Spring? Now's the time
when power either blinks or doubles down.

Uncle Vin on Spring

I like the early part, before it gets
all gussied up with birds and flowers. March,
you know? Snow, wind, rain,
the whole nine yards of weather. Air
that's been, like, charcoal-filtered—no
tars and nicotine, you know? Down the park?
Big trees wearin' cammies, bark
peeling in gray and yellow blotches. You
want birds? What the hey:
throw in a couple or three or four starlings,
green-black in front, what a freakin' paint job!
Ball field's defrosting. Snow still melting
in straightaway center. Right field's a swamp. Batter
wearin' winter gloves, you kidding? It
hurts to hit that sucker, especially with them
aluminum bats, gimmeabreak.
                          Next thing you know
it's April. Forsythia. Daffodils.
Whatchamacallems. Far as I'm concerned,
they can roll out the tarp. The whole freakin' place
looks like the lingerie department.

Langur Monkeys in a Fig Tree: a Photograph

As if transfigured, or
wired in series, the
last one's looped tail
tapping into the moon's
pale wattage, they
squat, owlish and
incandescent, on
invisible limb, ears
bristling, black
on black: a
zinc-filament silhouette, a
four-headed phantom, a
ciliated bolt of lightning.

April

Why talk superlatives? Each month is cruel
in its own bemusing, diabolic way.
Whose heart remains unscathed by the ides of May?
the indecencies of June? Who is such a fool
as to misconstrue September's smoky haze?
October's crimson valedictory?
The black-and-white cinematography
of November? December's pinched, astringent days?
April's cruelty consists—But what the hey?
Why parse the way it spawns, then brings to grief
the little eggs of hope? throws into relief
our sorry duffel of mortality?
The cruelest month? Don't even ask, What is it?
Just be thankful for its latest visit.

Cropped Limes

New shoots grace the amputated limes
we said wouldn't grow. Hardly a month ago
their lopped boughs under patina of rime
confounded hope. These hat racks for snow
could only wither in their plots. . . . Now, at home
with the whip and tang of April in the air,
those limbs like broken bones or stilted poems
inspire and embarrass us to care
for what's easier still to denigrate: ourselves—
colt-legged, too ugly even to tease,
aspirations moldering on the shelf.
These trees are tough: tough enough to freeze
like Catholic girls in knee socks in the snow,
then, sunstruck, to forget their prayers and grow.

Mnemonic

The medical equipment
technician delivering the
oxygen tank my
emphysemic father
needs to help him
recover from the
exertion of walking from
one room to the next
is coaching him on how
much time to allot
each half of the
inhale-exhale cycle.
Here's the deal,
he says, demonstrating.
Inhale: "Smell the flowers."
Exhale: "Blow out the candle."

May

If you were a college student, you'd be home now,
spring and summer stretching out ahead
like a westbound freight, a honky-tonker's bed,
a sweetheart's unpremeditated vow.
But even as these tropes, when scratched and sniffed,
harbor disappointments; even as youth,
which seems an unadulterated gift,
is fretted by its own serrated tooth;
so May, for all its amber/lemon/lime
leaves, breezy scents and vestal light,
disappoints: charms by day, chafes by night;
massages, and distorts, our sense of time;
strokes our mooning face, then just for spite
smacks us one; nuzzles, fawns—and bites.

Traditional Air

She sang an air in Gaelic of a selkie
who forsook the sea for love, reared a child,
then let the waves reclaim her. And a song
of a laborer who stopped to buy a drink
and "left his rent in his throat." She diddle-deed
a jig, a slip jig, a reel in quick succession,
her voice a Sligo fiddle bright with trills,
triplets, inflections, the melodies making
the spine tingle as she scaled the upper registers.
A fiddler myself (she'd heard my set and liked it),
I was smitten. Asked her out. We dined, then toddled
arm-in-arm up Ninth, where I did my middle-aged
damnedest to charm her sox off. ("A" for effort:
She kissed me, caught the C to Far Rockaway.)

Sleeping in Kansas

Night falls. We take no chances, head
for the cellar, where the radio dissolves
in static; turn it off; try to sleep.
Quiet broken by the muffled tick of
moths sideswiping the Coleman.

*

Toward dawn the cyclone strikes, its funnel
tossing cars like jacks, spitting Chiclets of roof,
then veering, chasing tail across the prairie.
A bruised moon reappears, sets. The smell
of eggs rotting in preposterous sunshine.

June

Excess is excess. Mesmerizing at first,
then overwhelming—the aphrodisiac rose
blown, and ditto the apperceptive fuse.
A quadrizillion pheromones do their worst,
unhinging the animal world with each new burst
of chemical cues (nature's cleverest ruse:
its linking of the organ of breath—the nose—
with that of propagation). June's well-versed
in fragrances, colors, seduction stratagems
of every sort, their success never so clear
as when the flowering mimosa's pink and lem-
on shuttlecocks fill the air with drifting seeds
whose scent makes high-school juniors want to breed
and breed again. A reckless time of year.

Erhu Player: Central Park

Two tenor saxophonists commandeer
the gazebo by the lake. A bop quintet
is busking to the south of Harlem Meer.
It's New York City; jazz is bound to set
the tone, as shades of new green come alive,
ducklings hone their moonwalking routine,
citizens defrost, and tourists bike the drive.
But what to make of this other-worldly keen,
this shrill? A wizened erhu player stares
ahead and bows a solitary string. . . .
The bowed notes' eerie intervals, the bare
melodies, transmogrify a spring
morning into something sere and bleak;
the park into some Himalayan peak.

Montreal

Pastel townhouses, trim and window-boxed;
cabbies who seem unruffled by the loss
of precious moments to traffic lights: All's
copasetic here beneath the beaming cross.

You are aces on brasseries and cycle shops—
simple amenities that go far.
Your subways are hospitable as dormitories,
unlike New York's (which nevertheless are).

A good cheeseburger is hard to find.
But *Le Nomade* sells Tunisian tea in glasses.
A cyclist in Ray-Bans pedals by,
rolling up his pants cuff as he passes.

The very dogs here seem to pee discreetly.
But damn this airbrushed photo: Something's missing.
No one's jiving, cracking wise, cutting loose—
except one crank who rants at a couple kissing.

July

Summer shimmies in: cerulean skies;
greenery whose color's meant to last
(unlike April's lime); the silver cast
to the morning light; cobalt dragonflies
patrolling tracts of soporific grass
or treading water in the humid air;
the kids, just shut of school, with time to spare—
eyes glazed, thoughts encased in frosted glass.
Month of torrid afternoons, sweet
protracted dusks and the unexpected rush
of neon plumage darting from a bush—
an indigo bunting knifing through the heat
vectors, sudden as a high-school crush,
then gone the way it came: in a tripped heartbeat.

Community Garden

Low-slung magenta. A
    hoi polloi of clover.

Dun stems issue in unfurled leaves that
    cant like beach umbrellas above the color field.

Beyond the clover: razor grass and, in its midst, a stand of
    vertical stalks, each stalk torqued by the
        spear point of an unblown bud.

Six or seven stalks lord it above the rest. When a breeze blows,
    the grass and flowers rock in sync like robed
        Baptists in a choir box.

The tall stalks, all unspent potential and vegetable gravitas, barely
    move. Got cellulose. What's
        a little wind?

Giving It Up

Love, that crack cocaine whose highs
are stratospheric but whose lows
are benthic trenches, inky troughs,
is daring me again to fly.
By now I ought to know what goes
with taking up the pipe: the off-
the-charts rush that guns the heart;
the addled mind that otherwise
would muddle through, glum but intact.
Still, there's an intractable part
of me that can't say no; that lies
awake churning, insomniac,
night-swimmer in an undertow;
that gives it up to the god that gets it off.

August

The thrill is gone. Think trickling sweat and smog
alerts, hornets scouring the melon rinds
and soda cans. Oh, there are those who find
midsummer tranquilizing as a drug;
who cotton to the oven-roasted days
and basted nights, the intermittent trace
of ozone in the air, the languid pace
that caters to our listless, saurian ways.
But once those hulking Caribbean low-
pressure domes, their muggy edges fraught
with storms and tropical allergens, come to squat,
I grow antsy as a grade-school tot
on Labor Day. Something's brewing that I ought
to be ready to encounter, yet am not.

First Love

Remember you? Nope. *(Olive-green two-piece,*
white sweat shirt, tennis sneakers, chestnut hair
and eyes—horse chestnut eyes. Around the cheeks
and nose, a smattering of copper freckles—
"Buckshot," I teased, after Wild Bill Hickok's horse
in the TV western reruns we would watch
for laughs, the occasional rainy night. . . .
Blue blouse. Green shorts. Auburn butterfly clip
gathering blown-dry Herbal Essence tresses.
Irish wit. Unaffected laugh.
Ping-pong wrist. That thing you had for ice pops—
Good Humor blue-raspberry double-sticks. . . .)
Remember you? Just the August afternoon
you cut me loose. And then the Sturgeon Moon.

Odysseus, Suspended

Pick up the story at the point at which
treacherous seas have left him dangling
from a fig tree jutting from a cliff,
as the roiled water—his life?—goes spiraling
down Charybdis's atrocious maw.
How long does he hang there? Long enough,
let's say, to understand just what a raw
deal he's caught: practically the stuff
of myth, if you're prone to think about man's lot
in mythic terms. Odysseus is not.
A deep-dyed and unblinking pragmatist,
he's already disengaging from the past.
But now bulimic Fate is spitting up
that briny effluent. He swears, takes the plunge.

September

Meteorologists' nightmare and delight:
when superheated air begins to swirl
like a marriage going down the drain—fights,
brooding calms, infidelities, furled
identities unfurling, spreading out
and the world be damned; to swirl, then to suck
and swell, to feed upon itself, to flout
barometric norms, breach bulkheads, run amok
on a hemispheric scale. From wind and rain
to tidal surge, this category storm
wants round-the-clock monitoring: satellite
feeds, instrument balloons, reconnaissance flights,
enhanced digital mockups. . . . Don't let the warm
breeze fool you. We're talking hurricane.

Cicadas

It's not just the interminable afternoons. . . .
(The bees, their pollen put up, haven't a clue
what to be about; the flight paths of June
no longer appertaining, drift, as I do,
from pane to pane.) It's when the daylight sheers
and summer's death rattle skirls in the field
beyond the house. . . . Lying in bed, I hear
the in-, then out-of-phase crescendos; yield
to waves of panic glasses of warm milk
won't assuage, cool compresses won't quell.
I get up, go outside (the air a silk
cravat) to stare it down. The clamor swells:
Darkness audible. Insomniac rune.
Primordial, incorrigible tune.

Strolling the Cross-Country Course

Here, where sumac's Mesozoic fingers
flame, is where the cinder trail ascends
the mountain, meandering before it bends
and grows steep. A runner, should he linger,
would see blackberry hug a locust's trunk;
mulberry leaves—buckshot, specked with rust;
a downed ash with a milk-and-coffee crust
of lichen; wood rats in a patch of skunk
cabbage, vanishing where rotted logs
sport coils of bittersweet. . . . But it's a race:
The runner's spikes crunch cinders as he slogs
uphill, tendons taut, then mends his pace.
Eyes to the ground, he'll miss the cranberry bog's
red tide, the aspens shimmying in place. . . .

October

Too soon to ring a dark, autumnal theme:
Here's sumac, goldenrod, a stand of pine
lit by flaming tupelos. Such benign
weather—crisp, sunny, dry—it seems
a shame to do anything but hoist a thumb,
hitch a ride, find a stream, toss in a line,
peruse your wiggling toes and, after din-
ing on blackberries, cashews, Jarlsberg cheese and plum-
apple cobbler (sack lunch of the gods),
roll the bag into a ball and crook an eye
at everything that's contrived to beat the odds:
the peach tree bent with sunset-colored fruit;
the grackles diligently scarfing crumbs;
the acorn-freighted squirrel on the fly.

Pausing from Chores

Grackles chuff and dicker in the boxwood.
Recollections smolder and ignite:
the infrareds of sourwood and sweetgum; smoked
aroma of October in the foothills of the Catskills.

This is how it was in Peekskill: rabbits
plundering at the crack of dawn; thermoses, books
cluttering the kitchen table; everything
lost, found, happening, waiting to happen.

High time we were waterproofing boots now, saddle-soaping
the leathers. Snow, if it jumps the gun, won't overwhelm.
The kids are pitching crabapples from the driveway,
hyperglycemic, tickled to be home.

Out back, the woods are quiet. A squirrel, face full of acorn,
freezes, sniffs the wind, then scrambles on.

Still Life with Soaking Dentures

for George Christophersen, 1911–2002

The eyesight gone—glaucoma and a botched
cataract operation. The hearing impaired
to the point where communicating is a chore.
The plumbing shot—a catheter and pouch
in lieu of the unfeasible surgery.
The black spot on the x-ray of the lung
that emphysema turned to sodden mush
years ago. The wheelchair he declined
until he could no longer use a cane
to navigate from bed to chair to loo.
The oxygen tank to which his body's tethered
24/7. The pharmacopoeia
arrayed around his orange juice and toast.
The withered husk that won't give up the ghost.

November

Month of abrupt silhouettes, taut verticals,
tossed branches parrying the season's gusts:
when lush gives way to stark, and technicolor
fades to black and white juiced by the dark
flame of a Norway spruce or the isolate
willow's incandescent filaments;
when the haggard skulls of hornets' nests once hid
by foliage of ash and elm and oak
heave baldly into view, and squirrels zip,
brash enough, through windrows only to freeze
halfway up a honey locust's trunk.
Month of brusque unveiling, giving the lie
to every hope not winterized in full,
not steeled against the worst: Stiffen our spines.

The Watch

All night, dun moths ghost-danced round the porch light.
Iced water went lukewarm; tea, cold. Well-wishers'
flowers wilted. During the wee hours,
the clock's diagonal shadow seemed to grow.
Night fears unleveled me. And you?
Now you blaze awake. A visitation?
Beside yourself with pain? Delirious?
Spellbound by the kind of predawn dream
that churns and churns, dust devil leveling
a straw stack? Dad, your panic needn't go
unspoken. Grab a hand? Or will you feign
control, the way a spent contender feints
and rolls beneath a roundhouse, buying time
for eyes that burn like meteors, or cinders?

My Father's Hand

He wrote as if ruled lines
were live wires. His
words—whisked lariats,
geese in flight—
blew through the white
corridors. We
stared, bug-eyed, then
emulated his hand and
learned at last to
read him as he wrote:
between the lines.

December

Zero degrees Fahrenheit, though far
from absolute zero—the state where atoms stop
their compulsive quivering and go to sleep—
is cold enough to give the dimmest star
a hard-edged clarity it will not keep
when the mercury inches up past freezing. Drop
whatever you're doing. Let the tea steep,
untasted, in the pot. Don your top-
coat, gloves and earmuffs. Venture out
to see this circuit board of a winter sky
whose every supercooled, glinting drop
of solder primes and focuses the eye.
Connect the dots till your neck muscles cry
uncle; till your soul extrudes and shouts.

Old Book

These days my memory's a looted library.
My neighbor's son's name, sister's street address,
the poem I spent the better part of a year
getting by heart—Where have the damn things gone?
PIN numbers, passwords . . . Yet the lower shelves,
the picture books: They're still intact. In the oldest,
I've woken from a nightmare, and my father
is walking me back and forth in our first apartment,
patting my back, saying, "If we only knew
what's got your little goat . . . Bad dream? Earache?
But you know what? That'll change soon. You'll be talking,
telling us what's wrong. And then, you know,
we'll sit down in the grandma chair, the two of us,
and clear the whole thing up. Won't that be swell?"

New Year's Eve

It's dusk, and the grackles are raising a ruckus near the
scrub pines on the university's southwest lawn.
Such urgent yakking. As if they've never seen night fall, or
found their families again after a day in the worm field.
Many New Year's Eves I too have felt
the crescendo of anxiety that comes with knowing things
are winding down. Opportunities, for instance—
the time for finding a less grubby job than proofing
copy and mechanicals for an advertising firm in Weehawken;
the time for finding a mate, and a perch less
shabby than my 121st Street tenement—bedraggled
lobby decorations, chandelier stolen over Christmas;
the time for rediscovering the peace that passes understanding,
which once descended routinely as nightfall, a luminous
clock face in the interim before sleep, a
father's voice phasing in and out of earshot. . . .

The birds can't get enough of the light, this last-minute confab.
I go home, make tea, listen to the radio reprise the
birth and death of rock'n'roll: the Orioles,
Elvis, Bobby Day, Dion and the Belmonts.
Midnight comes and goes. The radio raves on.

Milky Way

A man searches the forest for a path.
He slogs through marsh and underbrush, through stands
of hemlocks laced with windrows—as if hands
mountain-large, inebriate with wrath,
had pulled apart the hills. Such a grand
rooting up of trees and flush of light. . . .
Still, nothing like a path heaves into sight.
Eventually, the claustrophobic land
slopes to a lake. The sun goes down. Stars,
like eyelets circumscribing the deerskin sole
of a moccasin held at arm's length to a brand,
reveal themselves against the anthracite
sky. The lake's a carbon-copy scroll.
And on it, plain as day: a road of white.

The Seafarer

(translated from the Anglo-Saxon)

The Seafarer

The tale I tell is the truth; the song
I sing, my own.
                    Stooped over, belayed
to the stern oar, struggling with sorrow's tide,
I've borne breast-drought and bitterness;
steered keel through calamity's haunts,
the combers unfurling; coaxed bow
through night-narrows, numb, squinting
always at the cliffs I crept along.
My feet froze. Frost plied
its icy manacles. Miseries whittled
and hewed my heart. Hunger unmoored
my mind.
                    The man who's made his home
on dry land isn't likely to guess
how, hope-lorn, hagridden, bone-weary,
I've bided winters, weathered my lot
cut off from kin and caped with froth,
spellbound by the sound of waves
pounding the bergs. The blare of cormorants
was my harp, my hearth-song. No human laugh,
but the curlew's call, the cry of the gannet.
North wind's wassail. The nattering gulls.
The blast battering the palisades.
Then tern would keen and eagle scream
from frost-blenched throat. No friend hard by
to hoist a sinking heart.

None kens such caterwauling skreeghs
who sups in the burghs—no banished wretch
but a well-fed belly big with wine!
My burden bent me toward brine and thickest
night, where the North ungirds itself
in snow and hail, harrows the earth

with its cold seed.

                 Solemn thoughts
swell my heart, of the hurtling waves
whose surge I must withstand anew.
Mind-craving maddens; amazes; bids
soul strike out, seek the way
to a land that beckons beyond the flood.

No man on earth so might-proud,
well endowed, well arrayed,
strong of arm and staunchly backed
by lord but harbors a heart-churning fear
of the course the Lord has foreordained.
Forget harps, the having of rings;
women don't win him, nor the world's delights.
He longs instead for louring waves.
Sea-stricken. Sleep broken. Ballast awry.

Blossom and leaf, the light-drenched mead,
brisk trafficking in town and fair—
these but spur the seafarer
to cut the cord; to court fate,
inscribe his wake on water's slate.
The cuckoo coos in clenchéd voice:
summer comes; cares will ripen—
bosom's harvest. The blithe heart
gapes at the wilderness that woos
the plowman who plows the ocean-plain.
Soul, sprung loose from its skeletal roost,
stalks those briny steppes. The mind
delves, paces the planet's girth;
returns bone-dry and ravenous.

Eldritch, the cuckoo's call enthralls.
I'll gallivant in the whale's wake
that furrows the deep. Dearer by far
are the Lord's favors than this fell life
dealt us on land.
                    I do not know
as man's weal survives, world without end.
These three as lief would stem his tide:
ague, old age and edge of sword—
each one will let out breath from bladder.
So much for earldoms, earls, thanes:
You'd better have made your mark with untarnished
deeds; have died deserving renown
for what you've wrought and rendered, what
you've ventured in this vale of hate,
how far prevailed in the Devil's despite:
That those to be should bless your name
and angels declaim your epitaph
as the ages lapse. Leave such an estate
and scarcely can self be said to expire.

Empire ends. The emperor's hand
falters. Kingdoms come apart.
No earl bestows torqued gold anymore
like the open-handed lairds of old,
whose stout acts, storied graces
and burnished glories have gone by the board.
Those lords had pluck; would parry and thrust.
Today's pretenders bend or unbend
as best it suits. No brave man thrives
(quality won't out, but peters out,
putrefies the wan world over).

Age beards him, saps the blood from his face,
bleaches his hair. He broke his loaf
with warriors once. Not a one but molders
in the ground, a ghost. That grieves his heart.
Once vigor is spent, spirit wizens.
Nothing tempts or tickles him now.
He can't lift thumb or lighten thought;
tastes naught; can't walk; awake the night.
A man may bury his brother, strew
his grave with gold, but gold put up
won't ward away the wrath the Lord
God levels at a sin-laden soul.

Notes

"The Wheel": Chaney, Schwerner and Goodman: northern civil rights workers who were murdered in Mississippi in 1964 by local whites who considered them interlopers. Summer of Love: summer 1967, when an antiwar counter-culture coalesced in America.

"Krapp's Anniversary Tape": The title harks back to Samuel Beckett's play *Krapp's Last Tape.*

"If Your Dog Eats Grass, Do This": "[The grass is] the flag of my disposition" is a slightly tweaked line from Walt Whitman's *Leaves of Grass.* Bo Diddley: a seminal rocker.

"January": Armory Show: an art exhibition that introduced America to international trends in modern painting (1913).

"Wind-Chill Factor": Hell Gate: a current-plagued tidal strait in New York's East River.

"Milky Way": The poem's central image is taken from James Fenimore Cooper's novel *The Deerslayer.*

"The Seafarer" was awarded the 2016 Translation Prize by the editors of *Rhino,* the journal in which it was published.

An abbreviated version of *Where Truth Lies* was a finalist for the Tampa Review Poetry Prize (2018).

About the Author

Bill Christophersen was born in the Bronx and educated at Columbia University. He is the author of *The Apparition in the Glass: Charles Brockden Brown's American Gothic* (University of Georgia Press) and *Resurrecting Leather-Stocking: Pathfinding in Jacksonian America* (University of South Carolina Press), as well as three previous poetry collections—*Two Men Fighting in a Landscape* (Aldrich Press), *The Dicer's Cup* (Kelsay Books) and *Tableau with Crash Helmet* (Hanging Loose Press). His book reviews and critical essays have appeared in *Newsweek, The New Leader, The New York Times Book Review, The American Book Review* and *Poetry.* His poems have won awards from *Kansas Quarterly, Rhino* and the Robinson Jeffers Tor House Foundation, and have been nominated for a Pushcart Prize and for inclusion in *Best New Poets 2014.* He lives in New York and plays traditional and bluegrass fiddle.